D1479499

DISCARDED

PROPERTY OF
LOUISVILLE PUBLIC LIBRARY

Working Horses

Sharon Dalgleish

CHELSEA CLUBHOUSE

An Imprint of Chelsea House Publishers
A Haights Cross Communications Company

Philadelphia

PROPERTY OF
LOUISVILLE PUBLIC LIBRARY

J
636.1
DAL

This edition first published in 2005 in the United States of America by Chelsea Clubhouse, a division of Chelsea House Publishers and a subsidiary of Haights Cross Communications.

All rights reserved. No part of this publication may be reproduced or transmitted in any form or by any means without the written permission of the publisher.

Chelsea House Publishers
2080 Cabot Boulevard West, Suite 201
Langhorne, PA 19047-1813

The Chelsea House world wide web address is www.chelseahouse.com

First published in 2005 by
MACMILLAN EDUCATION AUSTRALIA PTY LTD
627 Chapel Street, South Yarra, Australia, 3141

Associated companies and representatives throughout the world.

Visit our website at www.macmillan.com.au

Copyright © Sharon Dalgleish 2005
Copyright in photographs © individual photographers as credited

Library of Congress Cataloging-in-Publication Data

Dalgleish, Sharon.
   Working horses / Sharon Dalgleish.
   p. cm. -- (Farm animals)
   Includes bibliographical references and index.
   ISBN 0-7910-8273-3
   1. Draft horses--Juvenile literature. I. Title.
   SF311.D35 2005
   636.1'5--dc22

                                                    2004016190

Edited by Ruth Jelley
Text and cover design by Christine Deering
Page layout by Domenic Lauricella
Photo research by Legend Images

Printed in China

Acknowledgments
The author and the publisher are grateful to the following for permission to reproduce copyright material:

Cover photograph: draft horses ploughing, courtesy of Australian Picture Library.

Australian Picture Library, pp. 1, 8 (top and bottom), 9 (top), 11, 14, 18, 19, 22 (top and bottom), 23 (top and bottom), 25; Corbis Digital Stock, p. 4; Getty Images, p. 20; John Hunt, Landcare Research, Natural Sciences Image Library, p. 24; © Peter E. Smith, Natural Sciences Image Library, p. 12; Pelusey Photography, p. 21; Photodisc, pp. 3, 6, 28 (left); Photolibrary.com, pp. 7, 9 (bottom), 10, 13, 15, 27; Photolibrary.com/Index Stock, p. 17; David Hancock/Skyscans, pp. 5, 26, 29; Stockbyte, pp. 16, 28 (right), 30.

While every care has been taken to trace and acknowledge copyright, the publisher tenders their apologies for any accidental infringement where copyright has proved untraceable. Where the attempt has been unsuccessful, the publisher welcomes information that would redress the situation.

Contents

What Is a Working Horse?

A working horse is like any other horse. It is a large, fast-running animal. Like other horses, working horses make a "neigh" sound.

A horse's coat can be any shade of brown, black, or white.

The adult female horse is called a mare. The adult male is called a stallion. The young are called foals. A group of horses is called a herd.

Wild horses live in a herd.

Mares

Mares give birth to foals. They will do anything to protect their foals. If danger is near, the mare snorts and neighs.

All horses are built to run fast.

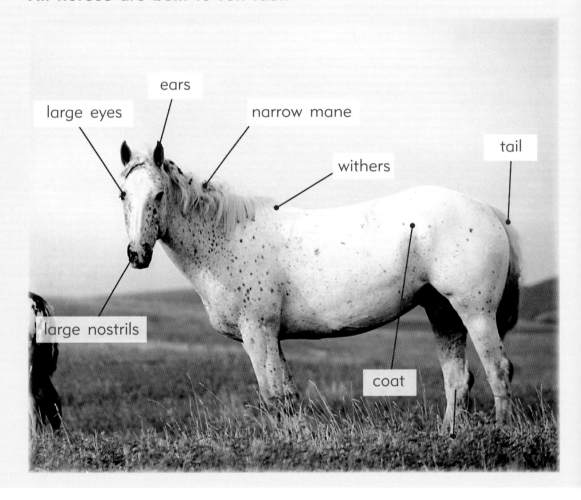

large eyes

ears

narrow mane

withers

tail

large nostrils

coat

Stallions

Stallions sometimes start fights with each other to show off. But they are not serious, and the weaker stallion gives up. They don't usually hurt each other.

This stallion is showing off.

large eyes

ears

narrow mane

large nostrils

withers

tail

coat

hoofed feet

Life Cycle

Foals grow up to have foals of their own, and the life cycle continues.

A foal is born with fur. After two months, it loses the fur and grows shorter hair and a long mane.

An adult stallion and mare **mate** to produce a foal. A mare gives birth to one foal at a time.

A horse is called a foal until it is one year old.

After one year, a young female horse is called a filly. A young male horse is called a colt.

Foals

Foals try to stand a few minutes after they are born. It is not easy for them. They try a number of times before they finally stand on shaky legs.

After one day a foal can run fast enough to keep up with its mother.

A foal drinks milk from its mother. After about a month, it starts to nibble grass. When it is six to eight months old, it can do without its mother's milk.

Foals drink milk from their mother until they are six to eight months old.

Farm Life

On the farm, working horses mostly live in a field. Sometimes they stand close together and **groom** each other by scratching and nibbling with their teeth.

Horses groom each other in the field.

Just as they do in the wild, working horses on a farm sometimes bite and kick each other to sort out who is boss. The boss is usually the smartest mare.

Horses bite each other to work out who will be the boss.

Playing

All the foals in the field get to know each other by playing together. Older foals move away from their mother's side and **gallop** and **prance** in circles around her.

Playing helps foals develop strong muscles.

Adult horses play, too. They chase each other and use their tails to signal to each other.

Tail Position	What It Means
held up	go!
held down	stop!
pointing to the sky	the horse is showing off

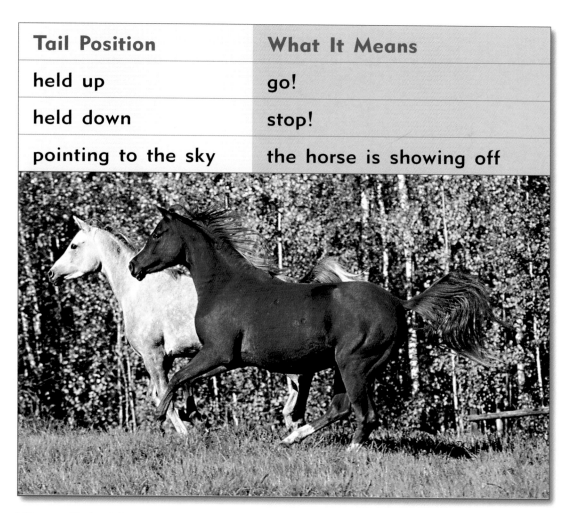

The tail held up means go!

Eating

Working horses eat grass. They spend most of the day **grazing** in the field unless they are working with the farmer.

When horses graze, they eat a little bit and move on.

Sleeping

Working horses lie down flat to sleep. They can also doze standing up. Special locking joints in their legs prop them upright and keep them from toppling over.

Horses lie down to have a deep sleep.

Horses at Work

Many years ago, horses did all kinds of farm work. Some farmers still use draught horses to pull heavy loads and **ploughs**. The horses wear stiff, padded collars.

heavy collar

plough

strong muscular legs

Sometimes, many horses are needed to pull a plough.

Today, most farmers plough with a tractor. But some farmers still enter horses in ploughing competitions at **agricultural shows**. Sometimes the horses wear fancy decorations.

heavy collar

horse brass

Horses sometimes parade in front of judges at agricultural shows.

Rounding Up

Some farmers use working horses to round up cattle on large cattle farms. Farmers also use motorbikes and helicopters to round up cattle that may roam over many miles.

stetson hat

reins

saddle cloth

leather chaps

lasso for roping cattle

boots

leather stirrups

In North America, cowboys on horseback once did the work that helicopters do today.

Horses make less noise than helicopters and motorbikes. So working horses are often used to guide the cattle calmly into the yards.

wide-brimmed hat

warm clothing

reins

boots

In Australia, jackaroos and jillaroos use horses to work with cattle in the yards.

Working Horse Breeds

Different **breeds** of working horses do special jobs.

The Quarter horse is the most popular cattle horse in North America. It can spring from a stop into full speed.

The Waler is a popular Australian stock horse. Walers were bred by early settlers. They are very hardy.

Some breeds are strong, and are used to pull heavy loads. Others are fast and can change direction quickly to round up cattle.

The Criollo is a stock horse from Argentina. It is very fast but can stop in an instant.

The Shire is a strong draught horse. It was once used to pull ploughs in the United Kingdom.

Looking After Working Horses

Farmers look after working horses by making sure they have shelter in bad weather. Sometimes, farmers move them to higher ground in case of a flood.

A horse in an open field can use trees for shelter.

Grass is all that most working horses eat. If there is no grass, the farmer gives them extra feed. The farmer also checks that they have fresh water to drink.

Working horses sometimes eat hay from troughs.

Grooming

Farmers only groom their working horses lightly, so their coats stay waterproof. Too much grooming removes the oils that help keep the horses warm and dry.

Body brush, to remove dirt

Hoof pick, to clean the hooves and check for rocks and loose horseshoes

Mane comb, to untangle knots in the mane and tail

Dandy brush, to brush the horse

Scraper, to scrape off water

Curry comb, to loosen extra hair and dirt

Farmers use many tools to groom their horses.

Working horses have horseshoes put on their feet to protect them. The shoes are made of metal and are attached to the hooves with nails. Attaching horseshoes does not hurt the horses.

Farmers check the horseshoes and remove any rocks and splinters.

Body Language

Horses communicate using body language, not words. Most farmers can "read" their working horses to know how they are feeling. They can tell you whether you should approach the horse.

A horse holding its head up with its ears forward is alert.

A horse with its ears turned back is relaxed.

How to Feed a Working Horse

What you need
- sliced carrot or apple

What to do

1 Hold out your hand so the horse can sniff it.

2 Hold your hand as flat as you can, with your thumb straight beside your fingers.

3 Place the food on your hand and hold it steady. The horse will eat the food off your hand.

Horses can only eat from a hand if the hand is held flat.

Farm Facts

- Horses are measured from the ground to the withers. Their height is given in hands. One hand is 4 inches.

- A pony is not a baby horse. It is a fully grown small horse.

- You can tell how old a horse is by how many teeth it has. A horse's teeth all grow by the time the horse is five years old. After that, the teeth just get longer.

- Horses cannot breathe through their mouths. That's why you never see a horse panting like a dog.

Glossary

agricultural show   a show where farmers enter their animals in contests and celebrate farming

breed   a group of animals that have the same set of features

gallop   the fastest a horse can run

grazing   feeding on growing grass

groom   to clean an animal's fur

mate   when a male and female join to create their young

plough   a large tool used on farms to dig up the top layer of soil in a field

prance   to jump around playfully

Index

J - 636.1 - DAL

Dalgleish, Sharon

Working horses.

AR: 3.6 0.5 pts Quiz # 85355

LOUISVILLE PUBLIC LIBRARY
Louisville, OH 44641

Fine on overdue books will be charged at the
rate of five or ten cents per day. A borrower must
pay for damage to a book and for replacing a
lost book.

DEMCO